ULTIMATE
EXPLORER
GUIDE FOR KIDS

By real-life explorer *Justin Miles*

FIREFLY BOOKS

A FIREFLY BOOK

Published by Firefly Books Ltd. 2015

Fifth printing, 2022

Publisher Cataloging-in-Publication Data (U.S.)
Miles, Justin.
    Ultimate explorer guide for kids / Justin
Miles.
[96] pages : color illustrations ; cm.
Includes index.
Summary: An authoritative guide written by
one of the few full-time explorers in the world,
to impart his wisdom onto the next generation
of explorers. Includes how to prepare for an
expedition, top tips on how to handle common
trick situations, and a look at every kind of
exploration, big and small, with diagrams and
images.
ISBN-13: 978-1-77085-618-9 (pbk.)
1. Discoveries in geography – Juvenile
literature. 2. Explorers – Juvenile literature.
I. Title.
910.9 dc23   G175.M453 2015

Library and Archives Canada Cataloguing in Publication
Miles, Justin, author
    Ultimate explorer guide for kids /
Justin Miles. —First edition.
Includes index.
ISBN 978-1-77085-618-9 (pbk.)
    1. Discoveries in geography—Juvenile
literature. 2. Explorers— Juvenile literature.
I. Title.
G175.M553 2015   j910.9   C2015-900491-8

Published in the United States
by Firefly Books (U.S.) Inc.
P.O. Box 1338, Ellicott Station
Buffalo, New York 14205

Published in Canada by
Firefly Books Ltd.
50 Staples Avenue, Unit 1
Richmond Hill, Ontario L4B 0A7

Printed in China

Conceived, designed, and produced by
Marshall Editions
Part of The Quarto Group
The Old Brewery, 6 Blundell Street
London N7 9BH
Publisher: Zeta Jones
Art director: Susi Martin
Managing Editor: Laura Knowles
Production: Nikki Ingram
Designed, edited, and picture researched by:
Starry Dog Books Ltd

DISCLAIMER:
You should NEVER put yourself in dangerous situations to test whether this advice really works. The publisher cannot accept responsibility for any injuries, damage, loss, or prosecutions resulting from the information in this book.

CONTENTS

Planet Earth is huge and full of awesome places to explore. With this book you can discover what life as an explorer is really like and learn some vital explorer skills. There are also plenty of ideas for mini-adventures that you can do right now!

This polar expedition was filmed for a TV documentary.

Polar explorers unload their gear from a helicopter onto the frozen Arctic Sea.

PREPARE TO EXPLORE!

The key to a great adventure is being prepared. If you want to be an explorer, you need to be fit, know what kit to take, and know what to do in an emergency.

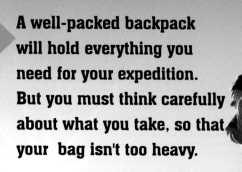

A well-packed backpack will hold everything you need for your expedition. But you must think carefully about what you take, so that your bag isn't too heavy.

Your backpack should be strong and comfortable to carry

TOP TIPS

• Carry a magnifying glass to look at insects and small plants, and a pair of binoculars to look at wildlife and to help with navigation.

• Use a camera to record what you see.

FLASHLIGHT

A reliable flashlight is essential. It's vital at night, but also useful during the day to see into dark corners and crevices. A wind-up flashlight is a good idea, as you never need to worry about the batteries dying.

You can also use your flashlight to send Morse Code signals. For example, to signal SOS in an emergency, flash three short flashes, then three long ones, and end with three more short flashes.

CLOSE AT HAND

Pack these items where you can get to them quickly.

- Essential kit, such as maps, compass, and knife, should always be in an outside pocket.

- Always carry a first aid kit (see below).

- Strap your tent to the bottom or side of the backpack.

- Carry a journal with you so that you can record your thoughts and experiences right away.

Be sure you have plenty of outside pockets for easy access.

FIRST AID KIT

Scissors
For cutting bandages to size.

Antiseptic wipes
Use to clean wounds and stop infection.

Adhesive bandages
Keep cuts and wounds clean.

Waterproof case
Keeps everything together and dry.

Gauze
Use to wrap around sprains.

Once you are ready to pack, clear a space on the floor and spread everything out. Now, arrange your gear into piles — one for essentials, one for clothes, and one for "if there's room!"

PACKING ORDER

Start at the bottom, and pack in layers.

Map, compass, gloves, hat, and cell phone in top pocket — TOP

Waterproof clothing in case it suddenly starts to rain

Lunch

Cooker

Food

Toiletries

Tent

Clothes and gadgets

Sleeping bag in bottom compartment

Flashlight, water bottle, first aid kit, and snacks in side pockets

BOTTOM

Packing bulky objects near the bottom will help your balance.

SNACKS

Granola bars, nuts, and dried fruit make tasty snacks and will help to keep your energy levels up.

TOP TIPS

• Make sure that you pack your rucksack the same way every time. This way, you'll know exactly where everything is, even in the dark!

• Leave a little space for things you may want to bring back.

AQUAPACS

Keeping things dry inside your rucksack is very important. Aquapac bags are great for this. You can use them for clothes, documents, or electronic gadgets.

Tablet in aquapac

You never know when things are going to go wrong, so you should always be prepared for emergencies.

Rope from your survival kit can be used to tow you out of the mud.

MATCHES

Waterproof matches can come in very handy. When you need to light a fire in a hurry, the last thing you want to be doing is messing around trying to strike soggy matches!

If you run out of waterproof matches, you can make your own. Melt some candle wax in a saucer, then dip the heads of some "strike anywhere" matches into the wax. When the wax is dry, store your waterproof matches in an aquapac bag.

SURVIVAL KIT:
WHAT YOU NEED

Don't leave home without a survival kit — a package of basic tools and supplies that could just save your life in an emergency. The kit should contain the following items:

Plastic box with a snap-on lid
To store your kit in.

Duct tape
For repairing broken kit.

Thin nylon rope or paracord
16 feet

Cotton balls
Ideal tinder for lighting fires.

Small wind-up flashlight

Penknife

Small magnifying glass

Whistle

A sealed bandage

Small compass

Foil blanket
For wrapping around you, building a shelter, signaling, or collecting water.

TOP TIPS

• Pack a foil blanket in all seasons, not just when it's cold. An injured person can quickly develop hypothermia.

• You can use a pencil to write HELP messages even when it's wet.

Pencil

Waterproof matches

A thin plastic poncho

Explorers often have to haul heavy loads for many hours every day, for weeks or even months at a time. You'll need to develop strong muscles and a healthy heart before your expedition.

EXERCISE FOR ENDURANCE

Exercise helps make your heart more efficient. It also develops your muscles so that you can work for longer without getting tired, and it helps to develop strong, healthy bones.

You should exercise for at least one hour every day. There are lots of ways to fit one hour of exercise into your day, such as biking to school or joining a sports team.

HEART RATE

Feel for the pulse in your wrist and count the number of beats in one minute. Now run on the spot for two minutes and check your pulse again. How much did it go up by?

Resting rate: 60–100 beats per minute

Exercise rate: up to 200 beats per minute

CAN YOU COMPLETE THE CHALLENGE?

Jump rope

1

Sit-ups

2

- **Perform each exercise for 30 seconds.**
- **Rest for 30 seconds between each exercise.**
- **Repeat the circuit five times.**

3 **Standing jumps**

Hiking up mountains requires a lot of stamina.

TOP TIPS

- Get your friends involved by playing games, such as tag, races, or team games.

- Don't use elevators or escalators—take the stairs and work your heart and leg muscles.

DRESS LIKE AN EXPLORER

You are likely to be outdoors for days or weeks on end, so it is essential to be dressed correctly. Something as simple as a good coat or a change of socks could save your life.

MAKE SURE YOU'RE ALWAYS CARRYING...

Sunglasses
To protect eyes from the sun, dust, and rain.

String
Very useful in many situations.

Spare socks
Carry extra socks and try to keep your feet dry.

Sunscreen
The sun can burn you even on the North Pole.

Winter hat __OR__ **Sunhat**
A woolly hat for the cold, or a wide-brimmed hat for the heat.

FOOTWEAR

A well-fitted pair of boots is essential for walking long distances, and will keep your feet in good condition.

Choose boots that give firm support to your ankles. They should be tough, waterproof, and fully lined with breathable material such as GORE-TEX®.

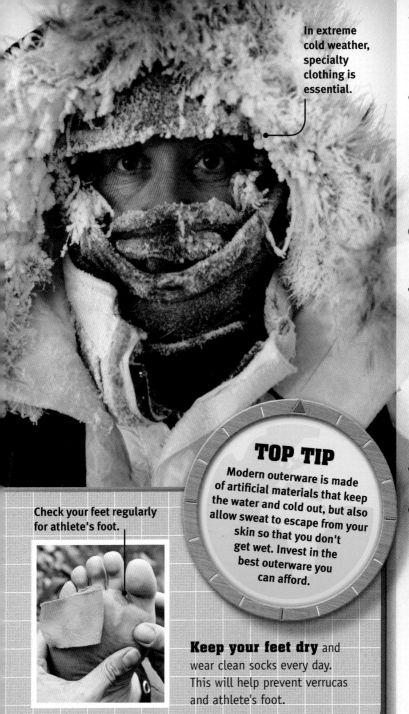

In extreme cold weather, specialty clothing is essential.

TOP TIP

Modern outerware is made of artificial materials that keep the water and cold out, but also allow sweat to escape from your skin so that you don't get wet. Invest in the best outerware you can afford.

Check your feet regularly for athlete's foot.

Keep your feet dry and wear clean socks every day. This will help prevent verrucas and athlete's foot.

EAT LIKE AN EXPLORER

Eating the right food is essential on an expedition, because we use up more energy when we're active. An explorer may eat more than three times the number of calories eaten by an average adult, and still lose weight!

Choose slow-release energy foods, such as nuts and dried fruit.

FREEZE-DRIED

Freeze-dried food is ideal for expeditions because it has had all the moisture sucked out of it, so it's light, long-lasting, and compact. To rehydrate it, you just add hot water, stir, wait 10 minutes, and eat — with no dishes to wash!

Freeze-dried meal in a bag

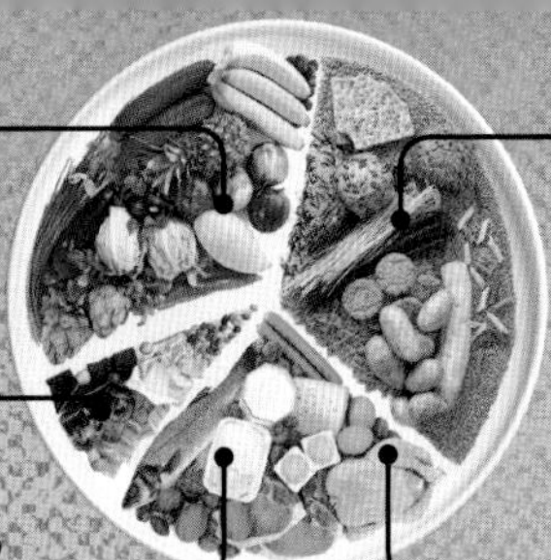

Vegetables and fruit

Grain foods

Fats and sugars

Protein — poultry, fish, eggs, tofu, nuts, seeds, and beans

Dairy — milk, yogurt, cheese

EAT WELL

To stay healthy, it's important to eat a balanced diet that includes foods from the five main food groups (see above).

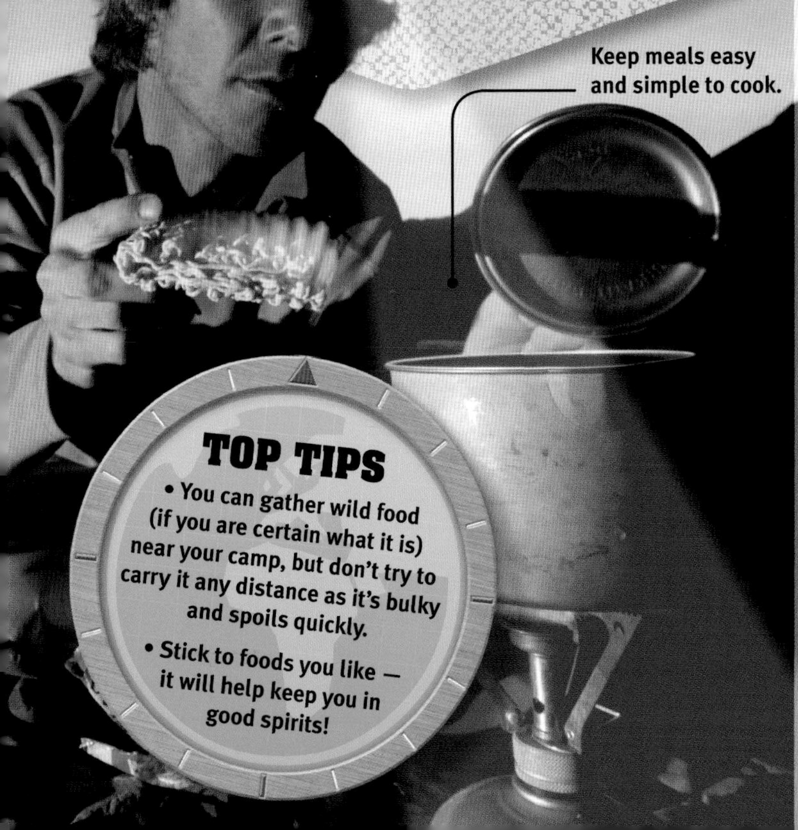

Keep meals easy and simple to cook.

TOP TIPS

• You can gather wild food (if you are certain what it is) near your camp, but don't try to carry it any distance as it's bulky and spoils quickly.

• Stick to foods you like — it will help keep you in good spirits!

Hacking through jungles, carrying heavy backpacks, or climbing mountains is thirsty work. Even in really cold places, you'll get hot and sweaty. So wherever you go exploring, it's important that you drink a lot of water.

HOW TO GET WATER IN
COLD PLACES

If you're in a cold place, such as the Arctic, Antarctica, or up a snowy mountain, you can collect snow or ice in a pot and heat it over your stove to make water for drinking or for rehydrating food.

STERILIZERS

Even if it looks clean, water can contain all sorts of tiny germs that could make you sick, so it's really important that you kill any germs in the water by sterilizing it before you drink it. You can use sterilizing tablets, filters, or a device called a steriPEN®, which uses ultraviolet light to sterilize water.

SteriPEN® water sterilizer

Try not to carry more than half a gallon (1.9 L) of water at a time.

TOP TIPS

- Have a drink of water before you set out — it's easier to carry it inside you than on your back!

- Plan filling-up spots into your route so you don't worry about running out of water.

COLLECTING WATER IN
HOT PLACES

When you're in the jungle, water isn't hard to find! You can scoop it up with a cup from a stream. You can also collect rainwater in a pot or from the creases in large leaves (see pages 72–73). But don't forget, before drinking any water you find, you MUST sterilize it first.

Wherever you are exploring, it is vital to know where you are and where you are going. Modern GPS technology uses satellites to tell explorers where they are, while satellite phones allow them to stay in touch from remote places. As a back-up, always carry a compass.

This mountaineer can talk to his base camp via a satellite phone.

MAGNETIC EARTH

Earth is surrounded by a magnetic field. The needle on a compass points to magnetic north. By aligning the compass dial with the needle, you can work out which direction you are heading.

Compass needle

WHERE ON EARTH AM I?

To find your location on Earth, you need two numbers. The first is your latitude, a measure of how far north or south you are of the equator. The second is your longitude, a measure of how far east or west you are of an imaginary line that runs from pole to pole called the prime meridian.

Prime meridian — North Pole

Lines of longitude

Lines of latitude

Equator

GPS

A GPS (global positioning system) uses satellites to tell you your latitude and longitude. The GPS receiver works out how far four different satellites are from it by measuring how long a signal takes to reach each satellite. It can tell you your location to the nearest few yards.

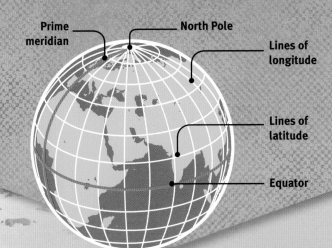

satellite 1

satellite 2

satellite 3

satellite 4

Distance to each satellite is different

Your position

You don't have to travel to far-off places to explore. You can learn and practice new skills on your doorstep—and then move on to tougher expeditions when you're ready.

CAMP OUT

The best way to find out what it's like to sleep outdoors is to set up camp in your backyard. It's a great place to practice putting up a tent and cooking your own food. If you forgot anything, you can just run indoors to get it — and if you need help, you won't have to go far!

WILDLIFE WATCH

One of the joys of exploring is spotting wildlife. You can do this anywhere outdoors — in a park, your backyard, the local woods, or the corner of a field. Wear dark clothing so that you blend in, take binoculars and a camera, sit in a shady place — and see what birds and animals you can spot.

Tawny owl

Keep a journal with maps and photos.

Fox

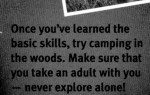

Once you've learned the basic skills, try camping in the woods. Make sure that you take an adult with you — never explore alone!

WARNING

Safety first!

⚠ Get permission from your parents before you go camping. Always tell them where you're going and when you'll be back.

⚠ Ask the landowner's permission before setting up camp.

KEY SURVIVAL
SKILLS

You're stuck in the woods. It's cold, night is falling, and your GPS batteries have died. So, knowing how to build a shelter and light a fire could just save your life!

Being able to light a fire quickly in the wild is really important. It can keep you warm, you can use it to boil water, provide light, or send signals across a valley.

You can make a spark by striking a knife against a steel rod. Wood shavings make good tinder.

5 WAYS TO
MAKE A SPARK

The hardest part of lighting a fire is creating a spark to ignite the tinder (see opposite).

Matches
Use "strike anywhere" or waterproof matches (see page 12).

Fire strikes
These are small steel rods that you strike together. They work when wet, and can be used hundreds of times.

Flint
Hold a piece of flint over your tinder and strike it, either with another piece of flint or with your pocket knife.

Fire plough
Rub a stick back and forth along a groove in a flat piece of wood. The rubbing action causes heat, which ignites the wood dust.

Magnifying glass
Hold it over your tinder, angled toward the sun. Focus the spot of light, making it as small as you can. The tinder will soon start to smoke and catch fire.

TOP TIP

• Stack rocks in a circle around your fire, or dig a circular pit about 2 feet (0.6 m) wide to light your fire in. This will stop the flames from spreading.

• Don't light fires without adult supervision.

WHAT YOU WILL NEED

To light a fire in the wild, you'll need three things:

Tinder

This is material that catches fire easily from the smallest of sparks. You can use flakes of birch bark, dry grass, pine needles, moss, or cotton balls from your survival kit.

Kindling

Material that lights easily from the tinder. Try small pieces of split wood, dry leaves, pine cones, or cotton rags.

Firewood

Once your kindling is burning well, add logs, branches, dried animal dung, or coal.

HOW TO TIE KNOTS

Wherever you go exploring, you'll need to know how to tie secure knots. The knots shown on these pages will come in handy in all sorts of situations, and you can practice them anywhere!

FIGURE EIGHT

1

2

3

This knot is a good stop knot. It can stop things sliding off the end of a rope, or stop the rope sliding through a pulley.

REEF KNOT

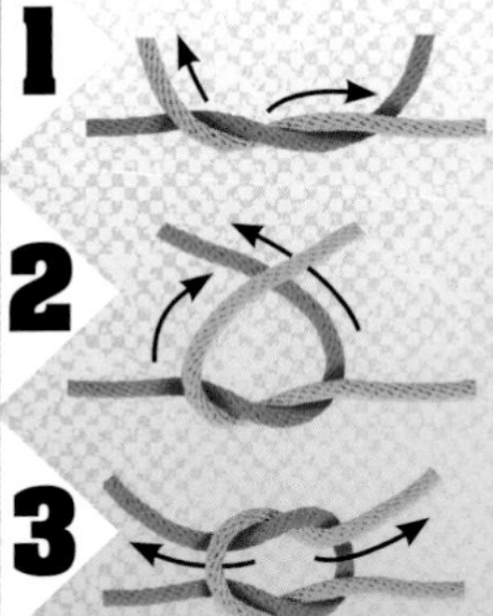

1
2
3

You can join two pieces of rope together with this knot. This can be useful if you only have two short pieces of rope and you need a long one.

TOP TIP
Choosing the right knot for the job is just as important as being able to tie the knot!

Figure eight knot used by a climber.

Mooring up

A clove hitch is used to attach a rope to a pole — it's a great knot for mooring a boat safely.

1 **2** **3**

Navigating with a map and compass is a survival skill that every explorer should master. Here's how you do it!

Lining up map features with the landscape

HOW TO USE A
COMPASS

Lay out your map **1**

1. Mark your start and finish points on the map.

• Finish   • Start

Place compass on map **2**

• Finish   • Start

2. Angle the compass so that the straight edge of the base plate makes a line between your start and finish points. Make sure that the "direction of travel" arrow (gray) is pointing the right way!

5. Now take your compass off the map and hold it level in your hand with the "direction of travel" arrow pointing away from you. Turn your entire body so that the "north" marker (N) on your compass lines up exactly with the orienting arrow. The "direction of travel" arrow is now pointing the way that you need to walk.

5 Direction of travel

Pick a point **6**

6. Pick a visible marker, such as a rocky crag, in the distance, and walk toward it.

Repeat **7**

7. When you reach your marker, repeat the exercise.

North Star

Plough

You can use the stars to find north. First look for the Plough constellation (also called the Big Dipper). Now, draw an imaginary line straight up from the end of the Plough. The first bright star you come to is the North Star. From this, draw an imaginary line down to Earth — that is true north.

Line up the orienting lines **3**

Finish

Start

3. Rotate the compass dial so that the orienting lines line up with the north–south lines on the map. Make sure that the orienting arrow (red) is pointing north.

4. The number that lines up with the "direction of travel" marker on the dial is your compass bearing — in this case 290 degrees.

Bearing of 290 degrees

4 **Your bearing**

Finish

Start

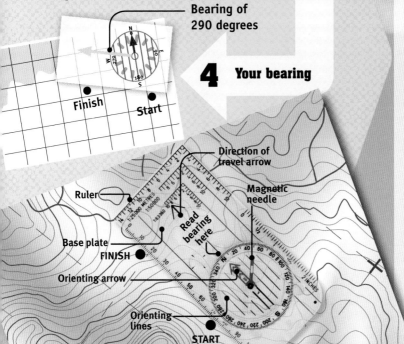

Direction of travel arrow

Ruler

Magnetic needle

Read bearing here

Base plate

FINISH

Orienting arrow

Orienting lines

START

There's a rip in your tent, it's getting dark and rain clouds are approaching — what should you do? Build a shelter! Try to make it waterproof and windproof.

Don't build your shelter too big. A small one will warm up from your body heat.

SHELTER SHAPES

Look for anything useful lying around nearby. You could use tree branches, large leaves, grass, rocks, bits of plastic, and rope. A knife or an axe will come in handy, too.

Igloo Cut blocks of ice and build them up into a dome shape.

One-person Tie one end of a pole to a post, drape a plastic sheet over the pole and weigh down the sides.

WET TEST!

Your shelter won't be any good if it lets rain in, so it's a good idea to test it out before you settle down for the night. Crawl inside, then ask a friend to throw a bucket of water over your shelter, and see what happens!

TOP TIPS

• Cover your lean-to with a layer of leaves up to 2 feet (0.6 m) deep. This will help keep you dry inside.

• Make sure that the entrance to your shelter faces away from the wind.

Lean-to Lash a pole between two posts. Add lots of branches at a 45° angle. Cover with leaves.

Leaf shelter Make a framework by weaving branches together. Cover with a thick layer of green leaves.

A-frame Lash two poles into a V shape. Repeat. Add a roof beam. Cover with a plastic sheet.

Pit shelter Find a ditch or pit in the ground and build a low lean-to over it.

Hammock shelter Tie your poncho to branches above your hammock.

EXPLORING EXTREMES:
POLAR
REGIONS

Some of the coldest places on Earth are found in the Arctic and Antarctic polar regions. A constant risk for explorers is falling through the ice. You have to be tough to travel to the poles!

The two polar regions, the Arctic and Antarctica, are quite different to each other, and offer their own unique challenges. Did you know, for example, that only one of the poles is on land?

THE ARCTIC

The Arctic is the northern polar region. The Arctic Circle begins at 66 degrees north (66°N).

More than two million people live north of 66°N, in modern settlements.

The geographic North Pole lies in the Arctic Ocean. The only way to reach it is to fly or walk across the frozen sea.

Arctic land mammals include musk ox, reindeer, caribou, foxes, hares, wolves, lemmings, and bears.

If you wanted to plant a flag into rock at the North Pole, you'd have to descend to a depth of 2.7 miles (4.3 km) to the ocean floor.

In 2007, this Russian submersible placed a flag on the seabed at the North Pole.

Arctic ice in 2012

Asia

North America

ANTARCTICA

Antarctica is the southern polar region. The Antarctic Circle begins at 66 degrees south (66°S).

Only a few scientists live in Antarctica.

The geographic South Pole is at 90 degrees South (90°S).

There are no land mammals in Antarctica, but there are marine mammals, such as whales, porpoises, and seals.

The geographic South Pole is on land — the continent of Antarctica. The continent is covered in ice, which can be up to 1.8 miles (2.9 km) thick!

Penguins live in Antarctica but not in the Arctic.

Africa

South America

Antarctica

Australia

When explorers start racing each other to reach a place, the risks and dangers increase dramatically. One of the most dangerous races took place in 1911, and the goal was to be the first to reach the South Pole.

THE TEAMS

There were two teams in the race to the South Pole. One was from Norway, lead by Roald Amundsen. The other was a British team, lead by Captain Robert Falcon Scott.

Amundsen

Scott (center, standing) and his team

THE RACE

Amundsen's Norwegian team beat Scott's British team to the South Pole, arriving there on December 14th, 1911, about five weeks ahead of the British team. Captain Scott and his team never made it back. They died from starvation and cold just 11 miles (17.7 km) from safety.

Antarctica

South Pole

Scott's route is shown in red, and Amundsen's in green.

Did you know?

In 2013, British explorer Maria Leijerstam became the first person to cycle from the edge of Antarctica to the South Pole. She pedaled her trike 396 miles (637.3 km).

THE SOUTH POLE

At the South Pole,

a ceremonial pole is used for photo shoots when explorers make it there. It stands a few yards from the geographic South Pole, which is marked by a plaque. This sits on glacier ice that shifts, so from time to time it has to be moved back to its correct position.

Ceremonial pole at the South Pole

ELECTRICITY

As a polar explorer facing extreme cold, you can't afford to take electricity for granted. Global Positioning Systems (GPS), satellite phones, and locator beacons all use electricity. But how do you keep their batteries charged when it's 30 degrees below zero?

SOLAR PANELS

Batteries are heavy and bulky, so you don't want to have to carry spares if you can help it. During the summer months in the poles, you can use a portable solar charger to recharge the batteries in your electronic gadgets.

Solar collectors mounted on a backpack

Did you know ❓

If you keep electrical gadgets close to your body, your body heat will lengthen the life of the batteries.

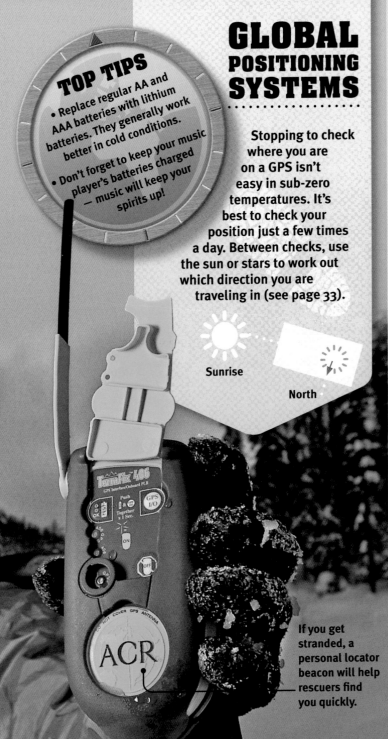

GLOBAL POSITIONING SYSTEMS

TOP TIPS

• Replace regular AA and AAA batteries with lithium batteries. They generally work better in cold conditions.

• Don't forget to keep your music player's batteries charged — music will keep your spirits up!

Stopping to check where you are on a GPS isn't easy in sub-zero temperatures. It's best to check your position just a few times a day. Between checks, use the sun or stars to work out which direction you are traveling in (see page 33).

Sunrise

North

If you get stranded, a personal locator beacon will help rescuers find you quickly.

For polar expeditions you need to be very strong, because the chances are you'll be hauling all your gear behind you in a type of sled called a pulk. Once the pulk is full of food, fuel, tents, and sleeping bags, it can be very heavy.

HOW TO ATTACH YOUR PULK

Pack your gear **1**

Attach a waterproof sheet and strap it down.

Load your gear into your pulk.

2 **Cover your pulk**

Attach two rope-like traces to the front of your pulk. These have elastic shock absorber sections that make it easier to steer.

Attach traces **3**

4 **Attach traces to harness**

EXPEDITION PULKS

Pulks used for expeditions are designed with high sides to keep things from falling off. They also float, which is important if you need to cross an open area of water, such as between the giant plates of Arctic ice.

Once you get it moving, the pulk slides along easily.

Did you know ❓

Explorers who trek from the Antarctic coast to the South Pole can suffer from altitude sickness, as the South Pole is 9,300 feet above sea level.

At night, it can be bitterly cold inside your polar tent. There's no respite from the cold on a polar expedition — if it's -58°F (-50°C) outside the tent, it'll be the same inside the tent when you first put it up. In the morning, when you wake up, it'll be a little warmer, but not much!

POLAR TENTS

Polar explorers often have to pitch their tents in high winds, on ice, so a good polar tent must be easy to put up. It should also have a ventilation system to reduce condensation, and have multiple air vents so you can breathe easily even if it snows heavily.

Tunnel tent — strong and easy to put up

Tipi tent — room to stand up inside

WARNING

Safety first!

If you don't use the correct bedding, in the morning you'll find that everything in the tent is covered in a thin sheet of ice. This is because evaporated sweat from your body will have condensed into droplets that have frozen.

HOW TO SET UP YOUR SLEEPING BAG

Insulated mat

1

Lay out one or two insulated sleeping mats on the floor of the tent.

Climb inside a BIG waterproof bag. This will stop any sweat from leaking into your sleeping bag and freezing.

2 Waterproof bag

Now wriggle yourself and the waterproof bag into a fleece bag, which will provide some extra warmth.

Fleece bag 3

Next, you need to get the fleece bag inside a BIG sleeping bag.

4 Sleeping bag

If it's really cold, put your sleeping bag inside another insulated bag!

Putting up a tent in the Arctic ——

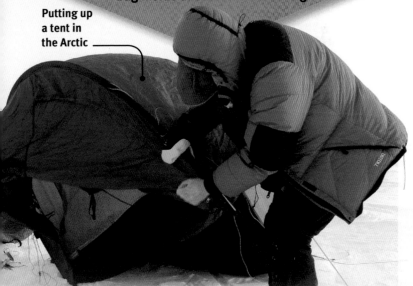

A good pair of boots is an essential part of any explorer's kit, but it's especially important if you're planning on visiting the polar regions — the most remote wilderness areas on the planet.

Your boots need to be big and strong to protect and support your feet. They also need to be light, super-warm, and easy to get on and off.

BOOT TECHNOLOGY

Boots designed for high altitudes and seriously cold weather are made from rubber and fabric on the outside, and have a gnarly sole to give them grip. Inside, they are lined with layers of felt to keep out the cold. An extra lining, called a vapor barrier liner, keeps your feet dry.

No sweat! The vapor barrier liner inside your boots is like a plastic sock. It stops sweat from seeping into the felt liner and freezing.

SNOW SHOES

You may find that your route takes you over huge ice boulders or pressure ridges. Attaching snow shoes to your boots will make these easier to cross. Like skis, snow shoes help to spread your weight, but because they are a lot shorter than skis, they are easier to move. Sharp spikes on the soles help provide extra grip.

SKIS

In the Arctic and Antarctic, attaching skis to your boots will help you to cross the snow and ice more easily and quickly. Skis also spread your weight, so you can cross Arctic sea ice without it cracking under your weight.

Did you know

There is actually a North Pole marathon — a full marathon at 26.2 miles (42.1 km), in which competitors run a route across the Arctic ice!

POLAR CLOTHING

In the bone-chilling winds of the polar regions, specialized clothing is vital to keep you alive. Early polar explorers wore heavy clothes made from wool and fur. Today's explorers use modern materials that are lighter and easier to move around in.

Polar explorers wear the same clothes day in and day out...

...it's far too cold to take them off! At the end of the trip, they **throw them away!**

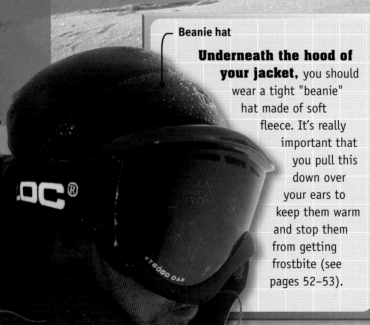

HEAD GEAR

Beanie hat

Underneath the hood of your jacket, you should wear a tight "beanie" hat made of soft fleece. It's really important that you pull this down over your ears to keep them warm and stop them from getting frostbite (see pages 52–53).

Outer gloves

Insulated, windproof pants

Polar goggles

1 **Base layer** — worn next to the skin — a tightly woven "thermal" long-sleeved top and pants (long-johns).

2 **Mid layer** — a very thin fleece undersuit.

3 **Extra mid layer** — a thicker fleece tracksuit.

4 **Outer layer** — a windproof jacket (plus a down jacket if it's really cold); insulated pants.

LESSONS FROM NATURE

Polar explorers wear layers. This mimics the way polar animals use layers to keep warm. Seals have a thick layer of fat and Arctic mammals have several layers of fur.

If a person's skin is exposed to freezing temperatures, it can get frostbite. At first the skin feels cold, then it may get pins and needles. Eventually, the area turns numb as the flesh starts to freeze.

BEYOND THE
PAIN
THRESHOLD

Sir Ranulph Fiennes

During an Arctic expedition, British explorer Sir Ranulph Fiennes got frostbite on his fingers. The damage to his skin was so bad, and the recovery so painful, that he put his hand in a vice and cut the tops off of his own fingers rather than endure the pain any more!

With treatment, skin with mild frostbite usually recovers fully. But if you get it badly, the tissue damage can be permanent and the end of a finger or toe may gradually fall off — *yikes!*

Outer mittens

WARNING ⚠️

Safety first!

Skin freezes to cold things, such as metal, very quickly.

TOP TIPS

• As soon as you notice any signs of frostbite, warm up the skin gradually. Tuck fingers under armpits, or hold dry, gloved hands over toes or nose.

• Never put frostbitten fingers into hot water.

Protect against frostbite by always covering as much skin as possible.

CONTACT GLOVES

Fingers can get frostbite very easily, so polar explorers usually wear two layers of gloves. The pair worn next to the skin is a tight pair called "contact gloves," made from lightweight material. They must be left on at all times to prevent the skin from coming into contact with anything. The outer gloves are usually a warm pair of padded mittens.

Find out what

it's really like to go on

an expedition

in sub-zero temperatures

with real-life explorer

Justin Miles.

(Q) WHAT IS THE HARDEST THING ABOUT LIFE IN THE POLAR REGIONS?

(A) The hardest thing to cope with is the constant cold and having to maintain strict routines to make sure that you don't get cold.

(Q) IS IT DIFFICULT TO WEAR LOTS OF LAYERS?

(A) It can get extremely cold, so every layer is really important — but I do miss being able to just wear shorts and a T-shirt!

(Q) HAVE YOU EVER BEEN IN A LIFE-OR-DEATH SITUATION?

(A) Yes, a few times! The most disappointing was when I was in the Arctic and had a massive hernia, which meant that I had to fly home for surgery. As I was pulling my pulk, the cartilage running down the center of my abdominal muscles, the mid-line on a six pack (if you have one!), split from the top to the bottom. This was very painful, but I still had to walk back to Greenland before I could fly home. The surgery that I had to repair the hernia really hurt, but with a new plastic mesh fitted to repair and strengthen my abs, I'm now fit again.

Q WHAT'S THE WORST THING YOU'VE EATEN ON A POLAR EXPEDITION?

A *Some expedition food isn't very tasty at all, but if I had to choose the worst thing I've ever eaten it would be raw whale tail that was given to me by the Inuit in north Greenland. Yuck!*

Q WHAT'S IT LIKE TO BE IN THE ARCTIC DURING THE LONG DAYLIGHT HOURS OF SUMMER OR THE LONG NIGHTTIME OF WINTER?

A *In the Arctic summer, when it's light most of the time, I can struggle to sleep. At night, the light wakes me up and I think I've overslept. In winter, when the days are dark, it's easy to forget that it's still the middle of the day when you're tired and want to go to sleep!*

Q WHAT DID YOU DISCOVER WHEN YOU WERE EXPLORING THE POLAR REGIONS?

A *For me, the most amazing thing about the Arctic is that when it gets dark, you can see stars from horizon to horizon in every direction and they seem so close that you just want to reach up and sweep your hand through them!*

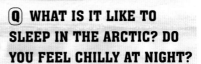

Q WHAT IS IT LIKE TO SLEEP IN THE ARCTIC? DO YOU FEEL CHILLY AT NIGHT?

A *I'm usually tired from a hard day's trekking, and this helps me sleep. I also have a HUGE sleeping bag that keeps me warm.*

EXPLORING EXTREMES:
HIGH
ALTITUDE

To reach the highest peaks, explorers need to master climbing and mountaineering skills. The challenges range from heat and humidity to freezing conditions and low oxygen levels.

THE SEVEN SUMMITS

Mountains can be fantastic and scary at the same time. The views are amazing, but the climbing can test your strength and endurance to the limit. Each mountain is different, and they all offer their own unique challenges.

THE SEVEN SUMMITS

Experienced climbers may attempt the amazing feat of climbing the "Seven Summits" — the tallest mountain on each of the seven continents. Opinions vary as to which mountains should be included, but a popular version is shown below:

Mount McKinley, USA

20,322 feet (6,194 m)

Aconcagua, Argentina

22,838 feet (6,061 m)

Mount Vinson, Antarctica

16,050 feet (4,892 m)

Mount Elbrus, Russia

18,510 feet (5,642 m)

RECORD BREAKER!

In May 2010, American explorer Jordan Romero became the youngest person to climb Mount Everest. He was just 13 years old. At age 15, he then became the youngest climber in the world to have scaled the Seven Summits.

TOP TIP

For each of the Seven Summits, you'll need to find out about training, equipment, expedition costs/sponsorship, summit routes, maps, guide options, best season to climb, documents, and immunizations.

Snow and ice are a challenge on all of the Seven Summits.

5

Mount Kilimanjaro, Tanzania

19,341 feet
(5,895 m)

6

Mount Everest, Nepal

29,029 feet
(8,848 m)

7

Mount Kosciuszko, Australia

7,310 feet
(2,228 m)

Above 26,250 feet (8,001 m), mountain climbers enter what's called the "death zone." At this altitude, there is not enough oxygen in the air for most people to survive, so they have to carry oxygen with them to help them breathe.

SHERPAS

The Sherpa people from Nepal have lived in the Himalayas for generations, and have adapted to cope with low-oxygen levels. They are great mountaineers, and their expert knowledge of the mountains has made them invaluable guides for Himalayan climbers and explorers. Today, the term "sherpa" is used to refer to almost any guide who helps mountaineers on Mount Everest.

Namche Bazaar in Nepal is the Sherpa capital.

Sherpas can climb with huge, heavy packs on their backs.

Did you know ?

The most famous Sherpa was Tenzing Norgay. On May 29th, 1953, he and New Zealand explorer Sir Edmund Hillary became the first people known to have reached the summit of Mount Everest.

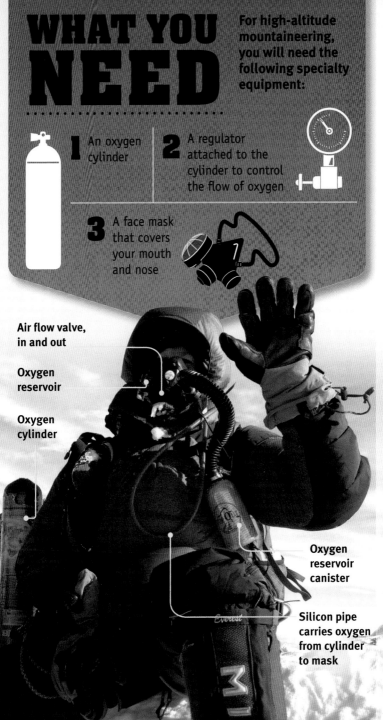

WHAT YOU NEED

For high-altitude mountaineering, you will need the following specialty equipment:

1 An oxygen cylinder

2 A regulator attached to the cylinder to control the flow of oxygen

3 A face mask that covers your mouth and nose

Air flow valve, in and out

Oxygen reservoir

Oxygen cylinder

Oxygen reservoir canister

Silicon pipe carries oxygen from cylinder to mask

In the death zone, there's 77 percent less oxygen than at sea level.

You may want to be the first to reach the summit, but climbing too quickly can be dangerous. If you rush up to a high altitude without letting your body acclimatize (gradually get used to) the lower air pressure, you may end up with altitude sickness.

DANGER SIGNS

Altitude sickness can strike anyone, even expert mountaineers. Often, people don't realize straight away that they have it. These are the symptoms:

 Headache Dizziness

 Exhaustion Sickness

You risk getting altitude sickness above 8,000 feet (2,438 m), but more severe symptoms generally occur above 12,000 feet (3,658 m).

An exhausted climber rests so his body can acclimatize to the altitude.

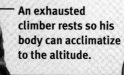

HELICOPTER RESCUE

In an emergency, if you think you might have altitude sickness, you MUST stop and rest, and let your body acclimatize. Then try to descend to a lower level. If you are very unwell, call for help. Rescue helicopters are used to fly climbers to safety.

A mountaineer takes it slow on a steep ascent.

TAKE IT EASY!

To make sure that you're acclimatizing properly to the altitude, it may be necessary to progress very slowly. This can feel quite frustrating. But even though your feet will be moving slowly, you'll be breathing faster and your heart will be beating faster in order to make up for the lack of oxygen.

A sheer wall of ice rises up in front of you, slippery and dangerous. There's no safe route to the left or right — the only way is up! Fortunately, you have the right kit for an ice climb — crampons, harness, ropes, and an ice axe.

CRAMPONS
HARNESS AND ROPES

Crampons are sets of very sharp spikes that clip or strap on to the bottom of your climbing boots. The downward-pointing spikes stop you from slipping on steep, snow-covered, or icy slopes. You can also kick the forward-pointing spikes on the toes into an ice wall to give you a firm grip.

Crampons clipped to boots

The harness straps around your body and the tops of your legs. Usually a climber attaches ropes to the harness using a figure eight knot (see pages 30–31). The ropes also attach to coupling links called carabiners that clip onto spikes driven into the ice.

Helmet

Rope

Harness

Carabiner

Ice axe

An ice climber uses an ice axe to scale the Hintertux glacier in Austria.

TOP TIP

The sheer drops and the thought of falling can be a little scary, but sometimes you just have to trust in your ability, the ability of the people with you, and the knots that you tie!

CLOTHING

On the highest mountains, such as Mount Everest, it's very cold, so mountaineers wear similar clothing and layering systems to explorers in the polar regions (see pages 50–51).

You swing an ice axe into the ice to give your hands something to grip on to.

Find out what

it's really like to go on a

mountaineering expedition

with real-life explorer

Justin Miles.

Q WHAT WAS THE FIRST EXPLORATION YOU WENT ON?

A When I was about 14 years old, I went on a bit of an adventure in France and that gave me a taste for travel.

Q WHAT DOES IT FEEL LIKE TO BREATHE IN LOW-OXYGEN CONDITIONS?

A It's weird! At first, you don't really notice that the air is getting thinner. Then you suddenly start to wonder why everything is getting a little more difficult and you don't feel as fit as normal.

Q HAVE YOU EVER SUFFERED FROM ALTITUDE SICKNESS?

A Yes! I've had altitude sickness once when I was climbing a mountain in Europe. When you get altitude sickness, the quickest way to make yourself better is to descend (go downhill). Your body has to acclimatize, so you have to reduce your altitude a little and then advance again at a slower pace to let your body adapt.

Q WHICH ARE YOUR FAVORITE MOUNTAINS TO CLIMB?

A I like climbing the French Alps because they are easy to get to from the United Kingdom, but they still offer some great challenges.

Q HAVE YOU EVER BEEN LOST ON A MOUNTAIN...?

A For the sake of safety and to save time, it's important to make sure that you know where you are and which way you're going. But having said that, I've not exactly been accurate with my navigation! I constantly check my direction as I move by using a GPS, a compass, or by walking toward a marked point on the horizon.

Q ...AND WHAT DID YOU DO?

A The trick is not to panic! Use your navigation skills to work out where you are and then start again.

EXPLORING EXTREMES:
WILD, WET
RAINFORESTS

Rainforest explorers have to be extremely tough. They must battle through thick undergrowth for days, avoiding poisonous frogs, stinging insects, and reptiles that may bite!

One of the first things that strikes you when you enter a rainforest is how dark it is. The trees create such a dense canopy of leaves overhead that very little light gets through. Anywhere that light can break through, a jungle of thick, tangled vegetation springs up.

An explorer uses a tool called a machete to try to hack a path through thick, thorny jungle vegetation.

JUNGLE

Jungle grows at the forest edges, along river banks, around rainforest lakes, or even deep in the forest where tall trees have fallen and shafts of light can reach the forest floor. Jungle vegetation can be so dense that it is almost impossible for explorers to hack their way through.

In August 2010, British explorer **Ed Stafford** became the first man ever to walk the entire length of the River Amazon from source to sea. The journey took 860 days!

Be prepared for wading through deep, slippery mud.

Emergent layer

There are four main layers of growth in the rainforest.

Canopy layer

Understorey layer

Forest floor

Did you know ❓

The biggest rainforest in the world is the mighty Amazon rainforest in South America. The second biggest is the Congo rainforest in Africa.

WARNING ⚠️

Where am I?

It's easy to get disoriented in a jungle or rainforest because it can look the same in every direction.

Creepy crawlies around in the rainforest, and the ground is wet, so the best place to sleep is in a covered hammock or on a canopied platform in a tree.

It's important that your sleeping area is covered so you don't get bitten by insects at night.

COLLECTING WATER

Finding water for drinking isn't hard in the rainforest – it rains...a lot!

I Look for rainwater in the creases of large leaves.

SPIDER ALERT!

Lying in your hammock at night, you may hear spiders dropping onto the cover above you. If you don't like spiders, this may keep you wide awake!

Venomous wandering spider, Ecuador

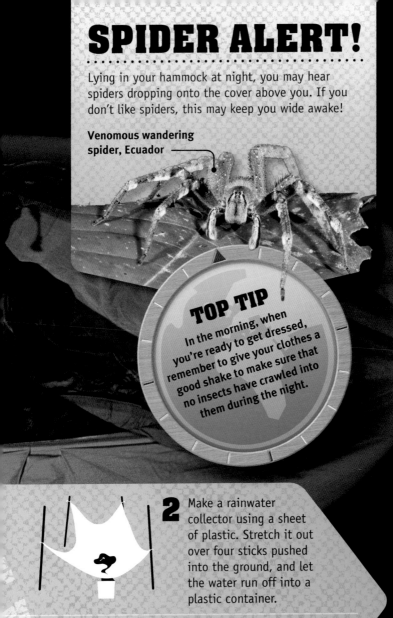

TOP TIP

In the morning, when you're ready to get dressed, remember to give your clothes a good shake to make sure that no insects have crawled into them during the night.

2 Make a rainwater collector using a sheet of plastic. Stretch it out over four sticks pushed into the ground, and let the water run off into a plastic container.

3 Collect water from rivers or streams. But remember the water may contain bacteria that can make you ill, so you must sterilize it using tablets or a special filter.

You'll need two sets of clothes for the rainforest — a "wet kit" to walk in during the day (this gets very wet and muddy!) and a dry kit to wear in camp and to sleep in.

WHAT TO WEAR CHECKLIST

- Loose-fitting, long-sleeved shirt. The loose fit makes it harder for mosquitoes to bite you through the fabric.

- Loose-fitting T-shirt made of moisture-wicking fabric

- Lightweight, quick-drying pants with zippers at the knees to convert to shorts

- Rubber boots

- Sandals for camp, to let your feet breathe

- Light socks

- A headband lined with tacky silicone to stop the sweat dripping

- A scarf or bandana to cover your neck

- Anti-leech socks

- Poncho

- Waterproof pants

TOP TIP

It's important to dry your clothes out as much as possible, because wet clothes can cause chaffed (rubbed) skin, which may get infected.

A wide-brimmed hat or baseball cap will stop water from running down your face.

Explorer Ed Stafford dressed for swamp and jungle trekking.

ANTI-LEECH SOCKS

The last thing you want are leeches (see pages 78–79) sucking blood from your legs. To keep them off, you can wear anti-leech socks over your normal socks and bottoms of your pants. Tighten the strings below your knees and tie with a bow.

Jungles and rainforests teem with an amazing variety of wildlife, from tens of millions of insect species to beautiful birds, reptiles, and mammals. Most creatures are exciting to spot, but many can cause trouble for the unsuspecting explorer.

JAGUAR

This big cat will eat just about anything it can catch, from tapirs and turtles to deer, monkeys, and snakes. It rarely attacks people. Look out for it in streams at dawn and dusk.

BINOCULARS

To spot wildlife, you'll need a good pair of binoculars. They should be light, waterproof, have good magnification (up to 8 or 10 times), and work well in dark places.

MACAWS

These brightly-colored birds are easy to spot in the canopy and emergent layers, where they live in noisy colonies. They eat nuts, fruit, and seeds.

POISON-ARROW FROGS

There are more than 245 species of these little frogs. Their bright colors warn predators that they are poisonous. A few species are very dangerous to humans.

BOA CONSTRICTOR

These large snakes, up to 18 feet (5.5 m) long, squeeze their prey to death and swallow it whole. Although a boa could kill you, it probably couldn't swallow you!

There are all sorts of creatures in the rainforest just waiting to bite you, poison you, or suck your blood. Tiny, poisonous frogs and huge, silent snakes lurk in the trees, leeches live in the undergrowth, and flesh-eating piranhas swim in the rivers. But more dangerous than all of these is the mosquito.

MOSQUITOES

Mosquitoes in the Amazon rainforest carry malaria and yellow fever, so you must take medication against these diseases. They can also give you dengue fever, for which there is no medication. To reduce the chances of getting bitten, wear loose clothing and apply insect repellent. You are most likely to get bitten at night, so make sure you always sleep under a mosquito net.

A mosquito sucks up human blood.

WARNING

Ferocious flies

The tsetse fly can give you sleeping sickness, and the sand fly can leave you with the horrific flesh-eating disease called leishmaniasis.

HOW TO REMOVE A LEECH

The damp undergrowth is full of blood-sucking leeches!

If you find a leech on you, which you most likely will, you can remove it like this:

1 Slide nail under

Slide a fingernail under the thin end of the leech to break its suction.

Push against thick end

2

With the other hand, firmly push a fingernail against the thick end of the leech, while continuing to flick at the thin end. Once you have dislodged the sucker, quickly flick the leech off.

3 Clean the wound

Clean the wound and bandage it to stop the bleeding.

Don't panic! Leeches drop off anyway when they have finished feeding.

TOP TIP
Check your body constantly for bugs and leeches.

After a sweaty day trekking through the jungle, you'll be hot, tired, and hungry. Jungle explorers carry freeze-dried food, because it's light and doesn't take up much space. But there's plenty more you can eat if you look around.

Preparing to eat in the rainforest of Papua New Guinea.

WARNING

BE CAREFUL — these may be poisonous:

⚠ Plants with white or yellow berries

⚠ Plants with leaves growing in groups of three

⚠ Plants with a milky sap

⚠ Don't eat anything unless you know exactly what it is.

HOW TO SPEAR A FISH

You can supplement your diet by spearing fish with a bamboo spear. To make the spear, follow these steps:

Cut bamboo **1** Cut a length of bamboo about 6 feet (1.8 m) long.

Separate prongs

2 **Cut two slits**

At one end, cut two slits about 6 inches deep to create four prongs.

3 Separate the prongs by wedging pieces of vine between them.

Sharpen **4**

Sharpen the prongs with a knife.

Spear a fish **5**

Hold the spear above the water. When a fish swims near you, plunge the spear in quickly. Try to pin the fish against the stream bed.

WILD FOOD

Look out for fruits and nuts that you may recognize, such as bananas, avocados (1), mangoes (2), figs, papaya, and cashew nuts. You may also find sugar cane, wild yams, and taro root (3).

Wild bananas

Find out what

it's really like to go on an expedition in the **hot** and **humid jungle** with real-life explorer *Justin Miles.*

Q WHAT'S THE HARDEST THING ABOUT BEING IN THE RAINFOREST?

A *Everyone's different, but the thing that frustrates me the most in the rainforest is not being able to see a distant horizon — everything is right up close.*

Q WHAT IS IT LIKE CAMPING IN THE JUNGLE?

A *It's okay — apart from the spiders! Sleeping in a hammock takes some getting used to, too, but it's better than being on the ground with all the insects.*

Rainforest spider, Ecuador

Q WHAT'S THE SCARIEST CREATURE YOU'VE COME ACROSS IN THE RAINFOREST?

A *Spiders! For me, it's always spiders. I'm not really afraid of anything...except for spiders!*

Q WHAT IS YOUR FAVORITE ACTIVITY WHEN EXPLORING?

A *I go kayaking and paddle-boarding when I get the chance, so I guess I would choose one of those. There's something really special about being on the water and moving at a nature-friendly pace.*

Q HAVE YOU EVER BEEN UNABLE TO MAKE A CAMPFIRE?

A *Lots of times! In damp places, making a fire can be difficult — and if you're just going to make camp, sleep, then wake up and start moving on again, sometimes it just isn't worth the effort!*

Q HAVE YOU EVER BEEN BITTEN BY A VENOMOUS CREATURE?

A *Yes — by a spider and by some sort of creepy-crawly bug insect in a jungle. The bite from the spider was on the base of my left thumb. It first appeared as a little pimple, like a tiny, itchy gnat bite, but within 24 hours I was in the hospital on antibiotics. The insect in the jungle got me while I was asleep. I woke up in the morning to find a trail of blisters along my arm. This is apparently where the insect injects an acid-like poison into your skin. When the acid has turned a small area of flesh into a liquid, the insect sucks it all up!*

Q WHAT ANIMALS HAVE YOU SPOTTED IN THE RAINFOREST?

A *I've seen monkeys and wild pigs, but no big cats — yet!*

Common squirrel monkey

EXPLORING EXTREMES:
DEADLY
DESERTS

Desert explorers are faced with constant dangers, ranging from poisonous reptiles, dehydration, sunburn, and heat exhaustion to freezing temperatures at night.

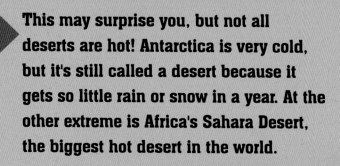

This may surprise you, but not all deserts are hot! Antarctica is very cold, but it's still called a desert because it gets so little rain or snow in a year. At the other extreme is Africa's Sahara Desert, the biggest hot desert in the world.

SCORPIONS, SPIDERS, AND SNAKES

Many types of scorpion, spider, and snake lurk under rocks or in burrows during the day to escape the heat. At night, when it's cooler, they emerge to hunt for food. Some of them are dangerous to humans, so you need to watch out!

A desert wolf spider emerges from its burrow, ready to chase its prey.

ADAPTATIONS

Plants have adapted to desert conditions in various ways. Cacti have a waxy layer on the outside to stop moisture from evaporating, and their sharp spines stop animals from eating them.

Waxy surface

Spines

Fleshy stem stores water

DESERT MAMMALS

With so little water, deserts are harsh environments for mammals, but many have adapted and thrive there. Hot deserts are home to mammals such as camels, fennec foxes, gazelles, and fast little jerboas.

Jerboas bound along on their long back legs.

The fennec fox radiates body heat from its huge ears.

Did you know ?

The desert with the hottest temperature ever recorded is the Lut desert in Iran, where a satellite detected a temperature of 159.3°F (70.7°C).

Deserts can be unbearably hot by day, so explorers usually shelter during the hottest part of the day and travel very early in the morning or late at night.

WHAT TO WEAR CHECKLIST

- Long, light-weight, windproof pants
- A belt, to prevent sand from getting into your clothes
- A long-sleeved cotton top
- A T-shirt under your long-sleeve top to control sweat
- A jacket for nighttime and to protect against the wind
- A wide-brimmed hat
- Sunglasses
- Desert boots

Desert clothes

WARNING

WATCH OUT!

When you're hot, the temptation is to remove clothing to cool down. But if you do, the sun will burn your skin, you'll sweat more, and dehydration — loss of body water — comes quicker.

SUNBURN

Sunburn is skin damage caused by the harmful UV (ultra-violet) rays from the sun. It's a huge problem for desert explorers. The first sign of it is when exposed skin starts to turn pink. The worse the sunburn is, the deeper red the skin will turn until, in really bad cases, the skin blisters and weeps.

British explorer Benedict Allen makes use of the cool of dusk to study his map.

TOP TIPS

• Even hot deserts can be freezing at night, so you must pack warm clothes and a sleeping bag for when the sun goes down.

• Wear sunscreen on any exposed skin.

There are many dangers in the desert, from sunburn, scorpions, and dehydration to getting lost in a sand storm. To avoid trouble, it's very important that you plan your expedition carefully and take precautions.

A sand storm approaches fast across the desert in Morocco, north Africa.

DESERT STORMS

Desert storms can be ferocious. As the wind blows, it picks up sand and dust from the desert floor, creating huge plumes of dust. If you see a sand storm approaching, put any electronic devices into plastic bags and take shelter straight away. When you're in a sand storm, you get sand all over you, and it's almost as dark as night.

Did you know ?

In 2006, Canadian runner Ray Zahab ran across the Sahara Desert — a distance of 4,660 miles (7,499.5 km). Each hour, he drank 4–6 cups (roughly 1 L) of a special sports drink, so he didn't dehydrate.

A desert traveler hydrates with regular small sips of water so as not to dehydrate.

HOW TO FIND WATER IN THE DESERT

When you're in the desert, it's important that you ration your water so that you don't run out. You can't just drink as much as you like whenever you're thirsty, or tip a bottle of water over your head to cool down! If you do run out, here are some ways to find water:

1 Search for cacti — you can suck the moisture from the stems. But remember, if the sap is milky, it's probably poisonous.

2 Watch out for birds, flies, or mosquitoes. Wherever you see them, water won't be far away!

3 Before sunrise, you can gather dew from plants or from under rocks by soaking it up with a cloth and squeezing it out into a pot or into your mouth!

Find out what it's really like to go on an **expedition** in the hot, **dry desert** with real-life explorer *Justin Miles.*

Q WHAT DID YOU DISCOVER WHILE YOU WERE IN THE DESERT?

A *As a boy, I always thought that deserts were just huge areas of sand with nothing living there, but I was very wrong! The desert is teeming with wildlife. There aren't many big animals, but there are tons of spiders (ugh!), snakes, small mammals, reptiles, and insects.*

Scorpion

Q WHAT'S THE TOUGHEST THING ABOUT TRAVELING IN THE DESERT?

A *I'm not a great fan of being hot, so I guess, for me, it's the heat during the day. The temperatures can be horrifically hot and, usually, there's no shade, so there's no escaping the heat.*

Q HOW MANY PEOPLE USUALLY GO ON AN EXPEDITION WITH YOU?

A *That depends on where I'm going and what I'm doing when I get there. My last expedition team consisted of ten people and my next team will be just the two of us.*

Q WHAT DO YOU LIKE LEAST ABOUT BEING IN THE DESERT?

A *Spiders, of course! After that, it's not being able to cool down again when you get very hot. That can be extremely uncomfortable.*

Q WHERE WILL YOU GO EXPLORING NEXT?

A *I can't tell you that! My expeditions are always kept top secret until just before I leave.*

Condensation process of turning from a vapor to a liquid, normally through cooling. When steam from your breath meets a cool surface, it turns back, or condenses, into water droplets.

Dehydration when the amount of water that you're losing from your body, through sweat, breath, and going to the bathroom, is greater than the amount of water that you're drinking. Even slight dehydration stops you from working your best.

Disorientation getting lost or confused about where you are.

Endurance being able to keep going, even when it's really hard. It involves pushing your cardiovascular system (heart and lungs), muscles, and brain to keep working even when they want to rest.

Evaporation the process of turning from a liquid into a vapor, normally through heating. When water boils, the hot water evaporates into steam (water vapor). Sweat on our skin evaporates into the air.

Expedition a planned and organized journey or long voyage with a purpose, such as exploration or research.

Humidity how much water vapor there is in the air. In places with a hot, wet climate, the humidity is higher than in a desert.

Malaria a serious disease carried by mosquitoes. Unless the disease is treated quickly, it can lead to death.

Navigate to plan a route, or travel along a planned route.

Satellite a human-made satellite is a scientific instrument that orbits the Earth. Satellites are used for communications, navigation, and to collect information that helps us forecast the weather.

Sterilize to remove harmful bacteria.

About the Author

Justin Miles is a professional adventurer and has undertaken expeditions and adventures in some of the more extreme areas of the world. His adventures include exploring the Arctic, climbing mountains, exploring deserts, and hacking his way through jungles. All of Justin's experiences have been used to support charities and to fuel various education projects.

Justin turned his passion for adventure into his profession after a car accident in 1999 resulted in brain injuries which left him having to learn to walk and talk again from scratch. It was during his recovery that he decided he would become a full-time explorer and use his experiences to support charities and inspire children to learn through innovative education programs. Justin is a passionate supporter of the global education program Educate A Child.

Acknowledgments

The publisher thanks the following agencies for their kind permission to use their images.

Key: t=top, b=bottom, l=left, r=right

Alamy
2br © Alaska Stock, 6-7 © Ryan Bonneau, 10-11 © imageBROKER, 11br © Stuart Forster, 12-13 © Kypros, 14-15 © All Canada Photos, 18bl © David L. Moore - AK, 20bl © Leon Werdinger, 28-29 © David Forster, 31br © Clive Tully, 44-45 © Alaska Stock, 46-47 © Nordicphotos, 55tr © ARCTIC IMAGES, 56-57 © Extreme Sports Photo, 84-85 © Edward Parker, 87tr © Matthijs Kuijpers 88-89 © adrian arbib, 90-91 (man drinking) © david pearson

Corbis
4–5 © Smirnov Vladimir/ITAR-TASS Photo, 18-19 © Braden Gunem/Aurora Open, 32-33 © Ted Levine, 35tl © Marcel Weber/cultura, 40cl © Hulton-Deutsch Collection, 40cr © Hulton-Deutsch Collection, 40-41 © The New York Times/ZUMA Press, 41tr © 176/Sallie Alane Reason/Ocean, 42cl © Christopher Herwig/Aurora Photos, 45tr © POOL/Reuters, 52cr © David Loh/Reuters, 58b (left to right) 3) © Colin Monteath/ Hedgehog House/Minden Pictures, 59tl © Michele Mcloughlin/Reuters, 63cr © Dimitri Iundt/TempSport, 72-73 © Richard Hewitt Stewart/National Geographic Society, 82cr © 2/John Slater/Ocean, 86cr © Nature Connect

Getty Images
16-17 Martin Hartley, The Image Bank, 22-23 John Lamb/ Iconica, 36-37 Martin Harvey/Photolibrary, 38br Stocktrek Images, 42-43 MCT via Getty Images, 50-51 Martin Hartley/The Image Bank, 52-53 Daisy Gilardini/Stone, 52bl (hand) Annie Griffiths Belt/National Geographic, 60-61 Barcroft Media via Getty Images, 62-63 John P Kelly/Photodisc, 64-65 David Trood/Stone, 68-69 Christopher Beauchamp/Aurora, 70-71 Stephen Alvarez/National Geographic, 71t National

Geographic, 71cr Guido Rosa/Ikon Images, 74-75 National Geographic, 80-81 Stephen Alvarez/National Geographic, 88cr Getty Images, 90-91 (background) Ladislav Pavliha/E+, 93c Frans Lemmens/ Photographer's Choice, 93br Kristin Duvall/The Image Bank

Justin Miles
1, 1t (inset), 3tl, 5tr, 48-49, 50bl, 54tr, 54bl, 55tl, 55br, 66tr, 66b, 67br, 82tr, 83tr, 92tr

Maria leijerstam
41cl

NOAA
38bl L. Murphy - NOAA Ocean Explorer

Photoshot
24-25 © Picture Alliance

Shutterstock
2–3 Marek CECH, 3br Morozov67, 8bl Silhouette Lover, 8–9 My Good Images, 9tr My Good Images, 10br monticello, 11cl Africa Studio, 11cr Richard M Lee, 12bl marekuliasz, 13tr irencik, 16bl Jenny Sturm, 17bl Patrick Poendl, 19tc Elena Schweitzer, 20-21 PaulL, 22bl terekhov igor, 25tr (top to bottom) 1) bogdan ionescu, 2) Mark Caunt, 3) Philip Ellard, 25br blojfo, 25br (inset, exclamation) Negovura, 26-27 Yurchak Sergiy, 29bl Jiang Hongyan, 29br Kucher Serhii, 30cl Maria Isaeva, 30-31 rtbilder, 31tl Yuttasak Jannarong, 31bc Yuttasak Jannarong, 32bl (map) Kvadrat, 32bl (compass) StockPhotosArt, 33tl tanais, 34-35 robert cicchetti, 38-39 Christopher Wood, 39b (penguin) Armin Rose, 39b (map) AridOcean, 46bl blojfo, 49tr Maridav, 49bc Kostsov, 52bl (warning) blojfo, 53bl pterwort, 54cr Roxana Bashyrova, 58c Godruma, 58b (left to right) 1) Galyna Andrushko, 2) Hugo Brizard, 4) Anna Maksimyuk, 58-59 Sander van der Werf, 59b (left to right) 1) Graeme Shannon, 2) Ignacio Salaverria, 60bl Zzvet, 60cr Vadim Petrakov, 62b Rosliak Oleksandr, 64cr Vinogradov Illya, 64bl Morozov67, 66cl Blazej Lyjak, 67tl Florin Stana, 71br blojfo, 72bl thobo, 73tr Dr. Morley Read, 75tr Giuseppe Lancia, 76-77 milosk50, 77tl (man) Pedro Monteiro, 77tl (binoculars) Jeffrey B. Banke, 77cr Redchanka, 77cl Dirk Ercken, 77br Patrick K. Campbell, 78bl blojfo, 78-79 Rolf E. Staerk, 79t sydeen, 80bl blojfo, 80br top to bottom 1) mkmakingphotos, 2) Seroff, 3) zcw, 81br Mizuri, 82cl Dr. Morley Read, 83br l i g h t p o e t, 88cr (background) Valery Shanin, 86bl 3drenderings, 86-87 Cat Downie, 88bl blojfo, 91tr Aleksandr Sulga, 91cr 3drenderings, 91br Aleksandr Sulga, 92cr efendy, 92b Galyna Andrushko, 93bl Olga Danylenko, 94-95 (background) Brykaylo Yuriy, 95br terekhov igor, 96 (background) Sergey Novikov, 96bl Zadiraka Evgenii

Troy Thomas
59b (left to right) 3).

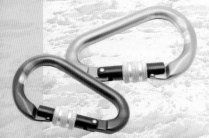